Once One Discovers Love

by

Caleb Delos-Santos

For Her

Contents

Don't Skip This.

No! Please, don't ignore me!
You claim to "love" poetry,
but, please, speak honestly.
You don't read it, really.

You skim these lines lightly,
dodging thoughtful study.
Truly, you don't like me.
You like feeling artsy.

You need "identity."
So, you sling poetry
on your *Insta*-story,
faking variety.

Don't hide your apathy.
I know you don't see me.

You really disagree?
Then, what's my rhyme scheme "G?"

Did you notice my syllable count?
Or, how it changed just now?
Or, how it returned again?
When did my "E" rhymes end?

No! Please, don't ignore me.
For once, inspect deeply,

visualize distinctly,
uncover my beauty.

Or,

feed your boredom and leave.
since I, like anything,
deserve someone who sees me.

And, if you can't be
that "someone" for me,
then, please,
stop reading poetry.

Several Perplexing Questions Following a Poetry Accomplishment.

Why don't I want to write? Why am I so demotivated? Wouldn't a highly likely or even possible poetry book publication make most writers continue brighter and mightier than ever? Why do all my current writing endeavors end in personal disappointment? Do duds unavoidably follow dubs? Fatalistically, is my recent victory temporarily stopping me from achieving something else of equal or even decently comparable quality? Or, does my likely soon-to-be poetry book harshly solidify my artistic peak? Will I reach higher feats? What if Destiny cruelly decides that my writing career needs to die after my one shabbily-done barely-fifty-page poetry-mess collection gets published? What if that hypothetical tragedy machine-gun-shoots me to anxiety-burning depression-churning creatively-crippling insanity?
Or, worse,
What if it somehow makes me happy?

Music Blinds No One Today.

Despite my trite max-volume-laden tries,
The Beatles cannot save my aching eyes.

Despite their scream-filled wheeze-trilled rehearsing,
Stringing sophomores cannot stop my sighting.

Despite God's steaming nearly-winter blow,
I am not blind to freshmen's mighty glow.

Despite their screeching month-old "adult" stress,
They beam intrigue, effort, and success.

Despite our fourth-year "opportunities,"
Seniors sleep, apathetic to degrees.

Despite my "need" to leave this noisy place,
I envy every freshman's fiery face

Since,

Despite my four-years-formed fine-tuned "security,"
I miss my glistening freshman vivacity.

And,

I wish similarly invested reckless energy
still lived within me,
keeping me
focused, lively,
and free.

Looking at Hills from High Above.

As I view this immortal plane of hills
While flying through polluted winds and sky,
The rustic browns of this dry-sea ground fill
Me with dread. There is nothing here. I'd try
To lie, describing this desert as rich
And speckled with eye-treats for the precise.
But on here, I can't. On this page, Truth, which
Kills all in the end, will project. A nice
Page that loves to lie would say deserts are
Serene. I say they're nothing, dead, unknown,
And scary. Deserts make me small. Like stars,
I am a speck of light in night. I roam
This dead expanse alive. I fly different
From the clouds I break. Nature does not like
Life. The dead are the shoe. We are the ant.
I'm living but weak. Soon, the dead will strike.

Her Hair in Acting Class Today.

As they relay
boasts on a play,
my sights survey
her locks' blonde spray.
Those slick strips ray
tint among grey,
sway dim dismay,
and make my day.

I Don't Even Know.

I like a girl that I cannot call mine
Since I have a "true love." Is it a crime
To care this much for one I cannot love
Romantically? When I dwell on this, doves

Circle my head. "How is this possible?
I have my person. My stomach is full.
She has filled my hunger for a best friend
To hold, protect, and care for till my end."

Yet, when I have this rationale, this girl
Storms my heart, like a twister, with swirls
Of doubt. "This girl is something else, the kind
Of love I wanted for so long." My mind

Cannot find common ground between these thoughts.
But, my heart wants the girl who stirred the pot.

Navigating a College Love-life.

Is this real? When was the last time I felt
like this? Where am I? Is this a dream or
reality? Where did these aches that pelt
my heart come from? Outside or from my core?

Why does my heart hurt in a realm I do
not know exists? If this is real, when can
I see her, who clean-cut my life in two?
What would I give to have us share one dance?

Would I go to Hell for cuddling this
new blessing in my life? If this is real,
did God plan my desire for one small kiss?
If this is fake, should I kill what I feel?

Does anyone, besides my God above,
know what the fuck is real or fake in love?

Beautiful Sludge.

Love is a beautiful sludge,
a bliss pinch, a gracious grudge.
Love is a shady porn site,
a sleek but scorned cyber bite.

Love is contradictory,
good, evil, healing, deadly.
Love is locks with lice, a ripe knife.
In a sense, Love reflects Life.

Life is a gorgeous corpse-heap,
clean, course, dreamed, forced, stripping, cheap.
Life and Love are everything,
which is dumb but encouraging.

I can be dirty royalty.
I can defeat "reality."
Like them, I can smite "sanity."
Like Life, Love, and sludge, I can be *beauty*.

I Love the Way You Dance.

I love the way you dance.
You never waltz. You flip
throughout the world and whip
its wars with your leg-lance.
I love the way you dance.

You never sit. You skip
and flick. And if you trip,
the plunge becomes your prance.
I love the way you dance.

You never nap. You grip
my wrists and sway. I slip
but never miss your glance.
I love the way you dance.

No Light Shines Quite as Bright.

Red Lights illuminate my **Love** tonight.
These **Church Freaks** screech to **God**. **She** sings and breathes,
authentically emitting different **Light**,
a **Flash** that does not burn but warms with ease.

Blue Lights ignite **My** edgy **Mind** most nights.
These **Flares** impair each **Positivity**
until **Her Purple Spark** explodes those **Lights**
with **Laughter, Hugs**, and endless **Empathy**.

Green Lights, sometimes, out-stage **Her Violet Rays**,
Limelighting Fears of **Loss** and **Poverty**.
But when **They** beam, **Her Light** from prior days,
which only spotlights **Peace**, gleams out of **Me**.

Fluorescent Lights shine everywhere today,
but **My Love's Light** glows every **shade** away.

Watching Worshiping While Churching.

Why do all worship leaders act the same?
They jump and jiggle on a flashing stage
while squeezing their mic and face like they came
straight to a bathroom in need of a change.

They march around, stretch their arms, and proclaim
God's name as they distract with vocal range.
My Love does not praise God like that, like fame
is her aim. No, she does not take the stage.

Instead, she gently sways, whispers God's name
and finds God in the church's back. Each page
of her notes sings her passion. The blind claim
she has restraints, but she has no such cage.

She does not act yet worships with no shame.
She does not jump yet shines more than the stage.

Her and Church.

I like to fight
Church and its might
or "light." Despite
my snide, her sight
replies, "you're right,
but it's nice." Night
can't eat her bite.
She makes Church bright.

A Sonnet on an Awesome Spotting.

Upon completing therapy, I peeped
my Sweetheart charting genius thoughts on her
absurdly fluffy fiber-back and gleamed
at classy plastered grass and tripped tree-fur.

I ditched the window, tumbling outdoors,
and scanned her land with pupil-perfect view.
Her plain mint blanket catered her gut-sores
with quick fry clumps and chummy chewy glue.

I tottered to her cute creative nest
and smooched her poofy mocha pasta locks.
I plopped into her pretzeled legs to rest.
"I love you," I said, spying her tech-clock.

I wish I skipped last Friday's writing class
and stayed in my Love's lap surveying grass.

Star Gazing on Our One Year Anniversary.

While peacefully reclining in your car,
Admiring this mighty "green" city,
I turned to see the sneaky love-lit star
that hides within your blissful eye with glee.

This quiet awesome cosmic entity
electrified my dimwitted kid grin,
distilling my one-day tranquility
with joyous Jude-like light inside my skin.

As that relaxing sun inside your eye
massaged my often shadowy psyche,
I thought back on our year below the sky,
realizing your light touched each memory.

The shine inside your eye ignites my hue
and always reminds me why I love you.

Star Gazing on Our One Year and One Week Anniversary.

While cruising droopily in my dark car,
Ignoring every wistful "winter" tree,
I turned once more to see your night-kissed star,
which still emitted bursting love and glee.

This silent lovely moon-streamed entity,
re-energized my tired adult grin,
evaporating my anxiety
with Jude-like love inside my heart and skin.

As that inspiring light engulfed my eye,
converting me to your glowing psyche,
I thought on future years below the sky,
realizing you will touch each memory.

The shine inside your eye ignites my view
and shows me why I will always love you.

I Love You.

I love you.
Thank you for every memory.

I love you.
Thank you for every mystery.

I love you.
Thank you for every rhapsody.

I love you.
Thank you for every victory.

I love you.
Thank you for every fantasy.

I love you.
Thank you for every comedy.

I love you
Thank you for every oddity.

I love you.
Thank you for every honesty.

I love you.
Thank you for every harmony.

I love you.
Thank you so much for loving me.

I love you.
Happy anniversary.

A Post Peace Pantoum.

Before my next depressive fret, I sat
in grass while passing lip-locks off to her.
That day, she cooled my core with precious pats.
Before, we swallowed scents and let love stir.

In grass, while passing lip-locks off to her,
I pried into her eyes with soothing tunes.
Before, we swallowed scents and let love stir
that past dull day before my future fumes.

I pried into her eyes with soothing tunes
that day. She cooled my core with precious pats.
That past dull day before my future fumes,
before my next depressive fret, I sat.

Pleading for Critique on a Monologue.

Why can't you speak to me more truthfully?
Each time I plead for artistic critique,
you string me nothing praises, like "it's good!"
Or pointless points, like "I like how you stood!"

Why can't you give me more than randomness?
Each time I try to pry for richer depth,
you sell me fool's critiques with empty cores,
like "your breath seemed too weak." Why? Give me more!

Why can't you tell me what needs work and why?
Please, think, "what lies behind each scream and cry?"
Perceive each line and choice delivery,
and voice each theme and subtlety you see.

Without the truth, I won't perfect my art.
Without your help, I won't know where to start.

When Your Girlfriend's Poem Is Better Than Yours.

You smile scientifically
with conditioned "Boyfriend" glee.
Then,
You twitchingly cringe slightly,
hiding wild jealousy.
Then,
You counter dramatically,
saying, "You're such a cutie."
Then,
You dwell on your morality,
hating your futility.
Then,
You think your life is empty.
lacking Praise or Infamy.
Then,
You proclaim Life is puny,
a worm in a galaxy.
Then,
You mourn Possibility,
which you killed with Frailty.
Then,
You reject Vivacity,
seeking deadly Ecstasy.

Then,

You stop, shift your thoughts swiftly,
and call your Girlfriend promptly.

Then,
You tell Her You are sorry,
knowing She felt your envy.
Then,
You smile genuinely
because your Girlfriend is heavenly
and better at Poetry,
Which,
You discover suddenly,
is incredibly sexy.

Hey.

You are the gold in the disgusting creek
I call life. Murky waters dragged my weak
pan through its muddy, deadly dirt pockets.
While there, stones launched into me, like rockets.

I bled in blackness. Rapids filthied me.
I tried to find wealth there. I did not see
much. I found some specks of shine. But, most flaked
away or turned out to be fool's gold, fake.

The river planned to keep me poor and cold.
Then, I rammed into a rare block of gold
that nearly blinded me with glow. The ooze
on my pan dried and died because of you.

My dear, I know how priceless you are. So,
I promise I am never letting go.

Hey, You.

Hey, you can relax.
You got this in the bag.
Your turbid pack of fears smears the facts.

Hey, you can recline.
One nap won't dream up eternal lag.
Your quick cruising mind won't stall behind.

Hey, you can smile.
Soon, you'll snag that last flag.
This ship brigade of busy trials won't stay awhile.

So, calm down,
Drop your frown.
Forget your Crown,
And maybe even
Clown-up your town.

But most of all,

Pause

And remember
Life isn't only
A storm of unholy strife and flaws.

It's also a breeze.

So, please,

Stop

And breathe.

Replying to My Love.

Last night, while sighting moonbeams, you sighed,
Love.
You hunted my exhausted eyes and cried,
Love.

While shedding, you pressed, "why do you want my
Love?"
Then, blankets ate you. I could not reply,
Love.

But now, tonight, my rhymes will tell you why,
Love.
Your feral feasting Love chomps my insides,
Love.

It daily stalks my heart and splits it wide,
Love.
But, thanks to such Love, I am still alive,
Love.

Because you monstrously brought me to life,
Love,
Your Love is something I will not defy,
Love.

Tongue-Twister-ing.

FuzzyWuzzy fan-favorites fittingly fair fur.

Betty Botter beautifies boisterous butter.

Peter Piper praises primed pulp pepper plucking.

Sally celebrates succulent seashell sucking.

Clams commemorate clean cream cans' complexity.

I scream. You scream. We all scream *Poetry*

Disguised as *Ice Cream.*

(:

The Big One 2.

Location:

A snow-blown or at least freeze-streamed sneaky tiny stony
Seasonally abandoned amphitheater,
Which harbors countless of our dreams and memories.

Music:

La La Land: "Mia and Sebastian's Theme," only the beginning, on
repeat.

Speech:

Squeamishly rises to speak
Weirdly clears throat
Two years ago, I wrote a poem/note called, "The Big One."

Pauses for proper yet somewhat pompous theatrical effect
Although I may not have shown this poem to your sweet sapphire
eyes many times,
You know what daemons possess those ancient broken rhymes,
Creeping peaceless fiends formed from over-thinking and anti-hoping
anxieties,
Which, even to this day, occasionally scream:
Suicide.

*Slightly holds to remind yourself to not fold or fiddle
with this pathetically printed silly little poem.*
Too much can happen between two years:

Sickness, health, poverty, wealth,

Pros, cons, more homes, less jobs,

Life, strife, wrists, knives,

Persistently dim agony and fright,

Resistantly shimmering peace and **Light**.

Goofily smiles while post-ironically pointing to your glimmering beauty

You

Happened within these two crazy years.

And, as you obviously know, that fantasy began on a common rehearsal night,

When I decided I liked you.

Of course, this decision whittled a beautifully new emotional cord within me,

Which played whenever you even remotely peeked at me.

And soon, I knew I had to pursue you,

Despite my music-less ties to another time-sucking love life,

Since you emitted a different

Light,

Frantically finicks with pants to reveal a last-minute purchased glow stick

Cracks it open

A flare that dared to defy every depressing rhyme I have ever written,

A flash of flare pants, *Starbucks* non-coffee chai drinks, and Baby Yoda hoodies,

Which passively clashed with every evil or even conflicting entity I had seen

Within those two broken years.

*Kiddingly clears throat again to substitute the jokeless dead
grass
And Wintry Colorado Springs breeze*
So, I combed my previously uncaring hair,
Strapped on my cracking black *Ross: Dress For Less*-bought soles,
And chased your glowing soul
With more might and hope
Than I have ever shown
In my twenty-one years of life.
Yet, silly me,
I should have seen that I could never reach you
Until you turned.

Tries to slyly chuckle
But once you did,
You burned every daemon away.

You
And your countering,
Bursting,
Unique,
And somehow
Comedically yet delightfully screaming
Love-lined shine of beauty
and vivacity

Freed me.

You and Your Light

Rescued and Brightened my Life.

Slowly flings shoulders and preps to bring it home
And now, one year from then,
Only one holy thing possesses my truly-typing poetic pen,
An awesome cosmic glowing entity
That daily relieves me,
guides me,
And currently
Inspires me
To silence each creeping anxiety,
Breathe in this charming star-streamed moonbeamed space and
energy,
And finally cease my talking
By simply shifting
And asking
Something
Big…

Question:
Gets down on one knee
Will you marry me?

A Lovely Chewy Cyrch A Chwta.

My Love is better than you.
Your greatest face can't brew stew
better than her smile's soup. Two
sips can unsicken a slew
of oozy sneeze days. One chew
of her chuckle can unglue
sour hours. She's my great food-tray
And one day, I'll say, "I do."

Hmmm.

Today, I feel happy.
It's weird feeling this joy.
Today, my words are sappy,
Like a love-stricken boy.

Today, my life is light.
The day itself is bright.
My sorrow is faded,
Or at least belated.

Tomorrow, I might fall
Back into that dead sea,
Where darkness surrounds all,
Where joy can never be.

Tomorrow could be bleak.
Today could be my peak.
Tomorrow I could die.
Today could be a lie.

But now, I will enjoy
This lively time of love.
I will laugh and annoy,
While in the light above.

Thinking About That Beast.

"When will I decide to liberate myself?
Why do I abide by his disfigured laws?
How will I escape or slay his shaking pelt?
What will Father say if I die by snide claws?

When will I decide he won't stop hunting me?
Why do I consider what he thinks about?
How will I dismiss his eye's enchanting gleam?
What will Father say when he sees my sleek doubt?

When will I decide his gentleness is bait?
Why do I enjoy his boisterous growling voice?
How will I ignore his horrid witch-stitched fate?
What will Father say when Love abducts my choice?

When will I redeem him? Why do I still stay?
How will I still see him? What will Father say?"

To My First-Grade Girlfriend,

I hardly remember you.
Mom said we kissed behind a tree once.

I remember the fading,
broken oak and its lover-drawn scars.

But, I don't remember you,
aside from, I think, your freakish smile.

It wasn't awful because
of its shape but its static nature.

It never faded or fell.
It only flared and flew, despite me.

I stuffed your still smile with jibes,
snark, and Dad's fart-jokes. Yet, you still grinned.

Of course, sorry for kid-me.
He, like most boys, treated you poorly.

But more importantly, thank you for your teeth.
These days, in adulthood, they remind me
to breathe gleefully
even when dealing
with bigger assholes than little-me.

Thank you, and please never stop smiling.

Sincerely,

Dear Brother,

On Our Hawaii flight three years ago,
I asked you for college advice. Although
I don't remember most of what you said,
one random quote has never left my head:

"Keep your door open."

Although you meant it literally, that phrase
consistently returns to me on days
when failure paves my paths. When struggles sink
My chasing feet, it cheers me up to think,

"Keep your door open,"

stay open to whatever God has planned,
including courses you don't understand.
You taught me to accept this test called Life
and welcome any wages, change, or strife.

"Keep your door open."

I really needed that advice. Thank you.
Thank you for always teaching me how to
survive Life. I don't know what else to say,
besides I love you and happy birthday.

Sincerely,

MOM.

Mom.
We all know the name.
Mom.
The word carries weight.
Mom.
We all know its fame.
The name for the great.

Mom,
The sweet and the kind.
Mom,
The most filled with love
Mom.
Whose passion you'll find
Soars past any dove.

Mom,
The one I latch to.
Mom,
On whom I depend.
Mom,
How much I need you,
How much you defend.

Mom,
Your name just for me.
Mom,
The one always there.
Mom,
One who'll always see
Us two as a pair.

Strong Dad.

I don't understand.
He's always so sure
When Hell's close at hand,
He won't even stir.

He has strength yet care,
Has care yet insight.
In all my affairs,
He proves he is right.

But, how can this be?
What makes him like this?
What truth does he see?
What gives him his bliss?

It will never fail.
That is all I know.
This gift will prevail
Against all my foes.

Peace is what it's called,
Which eases life's pain.
Peace is unequaled,
Peace keeps my dad sane.

Friends Seeking Dreams.

In dreams, places are often made up of fragments... in an unexpected combination...

What is it gonna be like?
I don't know. You can't describe it. Can't really put it in a box.

Is it supposed to confuse you?
It helps. Really makes a difference.

Look me in the eye and tell the truth.
It makes me feel like I'm coming into my own. Let's just explore...

So be it...

Old Dog, New Day.

The dog is fun today.
Most days, her face sprays dread
from her decrepit head.
Instead of spreading gray,
the dog is fun today.

A day ago, the bread
moved more. Today, she fled
the floor and begged to play.
The dog is fun today.

Tomorrow, something red
might not attract one shred.
But now, I can still say
the dog is fun today.

The Eyes of the Beholder

On Monday morning, my cat stared at me.
While in my desk chair, I dueled my pained head.
Caffeine would free it. In search of that key,
I found an ancient fuzzball on my bed.
I was then fossilized by that old cat,
Who has been in my home since I was small.
She's soft yet not smooth, fluffy yet not fat.
She's little yet scowls fiercely and stands tall.
Her fur is a grey rainbow of all shades.
But, her face is a dark and withered patch,
which carries emerald eyes. Those searchlights aid
Her gaze and make all, but me, fear a scratch.
She could have struck me, but she purred instead.
For in her awesome eyes, I am her friend.

To a Legendary Bear Named SUV.

No brother, mother, lover, or friend can
Mend my dulled tender soul, but SUV
Can. That non-man stands tall and cans all pain.
Insanely, thinking of him kills my woes

And builds a flowing well of joy that fills
My heart. That smart bear brings air to my teared
And fairly unrepairable lungs. When
Sad, a mad BH (Bear Hunt) chase makes me glad.

When dreaming, seething fiends of nightmares pry
Into my mind. But, fine and kind thoughts of
SUV "pastimes" toss nightmares to their
Ensuing doom. Above their tombs, the love

Of SUV creates great fated dreams
Of me meeting he who makes all pain flea.
Don't you see? He can set you free.
Undoubtedly, all should love SUV.

An Almost Summer Break Cinquain.

Today,
my trite Earl Grey
would taste greater in May,
When cross cagey college cramps stay
away.

Goodbye, Winter.

Goodbye, Winter. I
wish Summer's dumb sky,
which flickers too bright
and simmers too high,

would chill, flake, and die
so you can shine my
biography white
and bite my Goodbye.

Saying Goodbye to the House I Stayed at During Summer.

Goodbye, my Colorado summer home.
I'll miss your "pretty" eggshell walls
and every *Captain Crunch* crumb, pin, and comb
living within your prickly carpet halls.

Farewell, my summer safe house, where I fought
confusing online course assignments in
a box-laced basement on a stained couch-cot,
as rainbow blankets armored my brisk skin.

So long, my Colorado happy place.
I loved each lazy flatscreen day and fun
yet dumb "foam fight" hot tub night. Your "filled" space
saved me from "emptiness." Summer is done.

I have to leave for school. But, I swear my
best memories will live with you. Goodbye.

Here, Here!

Well, this is the end.
The break's final send.
The very last time
To make a break's rhyme.

It's been nice, the break,
Serene, not much wake,
More floating, more cheers,
Less drowning, less tears.

Passions were pursued.
Inner joys were found.
Most days were on cue.
Most rhymes were quite sound.

But, that time is done,
Floating in the sun.
Now comes those long days,
Where rhymes die in vain.

Time to say goodbye,
With a grin and sigh,
To the time above,
To the break I loved.

Autumn Cobweb Spottings.

Three cobweb spottings.
Fall's nature dreams and tauntings.
Bizarre and lively.

A sidewalk night light.
Popped strings socked fogged beams with might.
No spider in sight.

A red-ruled birch tree.
Snowflake hammocks gleamed fiercely.
No spider to see.

My cracked keyless car.
God's cloth glued the glass like tar.
Spiders flashed like stars.

Three cobweb sightings
Fall's nature taunts and dreamings.
Bizarre and lovely.

Hair Flowers.

Why do
flowers need to
tower hair? If plants grew
sound boxes, would they praise, snore, woo,
or boo?

Contact Conquerors.

Contacts guide my sight
but not like a knight.
No grace
focuses their fight
against blurry light.
They mace
grain, haze, shades, and bright
plains. They even smite
my face.

A Triolet About a Toilet.

A toilet is the throne for all,
the wealth, the daft, the schooled, the broke.
Unless you dwell where cars can't stall.
A toilet is the throne for all.
Unless your culture lacks *U-Haul*,
McDonald's, WiFi, *Bandaids*, *Coke*.
A toilet is the throne for all,
the wealth, the daft, the schooled, the broke.

Producing a Pop Star for Profit.

Silence. I won't hear your screaming.
Stiffen. I won't see your squirming.
Swallow. I won't feel your starving.
Snicker. I won't taste your sobbing.
Suckle. I won't smell your sinning.
Silly, we don't buy your striving.
Stupid, we don't sell your singing.

Things That Reach the Mouth.

TERMS:

Cooled Cola Can - Murky honey fizz in blood-burned metal

Blown-up (Cigarette) Bud - Bloated popped paper unknotted on stones

Steamy Shower Stream - Swamp fog mixed with metro machine liquid

Slurpee Straw - Stern flaky neon lake-blue sucking stick

Steal-skinned Six-shooter - Canine-filling gum-chilling brain-killing

MORE TERMS:

Sexy Steak - Perfect pricy juicy dark-hued steer-fruit

Aging Apple - Mesh rot spots scattered 'round heart-rounded flesh

Yummy Funfetti FroYo - Dapper dry drops folded in silk sleet slosh

Pale-eggshell (Plastic) Spoon - Snap-prone penniless scooper keeping soup

Air - Anti-asphyxiating gas rope • ! HOPE.

My Savior Above.

I find it hard to view the sky. That wide
hued spectrum chews into my eyes when I
try to enjoy its toying bolstering sides.
One time, when watching God's space-lake, I cried.

I shelved myself with pupil-saving shades
that day. And still, that gas-stained mass attacked
my irises. Last night, those plasma blades
invaded my sights with stacked back-up blacks.

The only hope against my foe has been
those planes. Each day, they tear that air abyss
with slick cloud zips. When I told my bulb-kin
to view wing-whales, they conquered cobalt fists.

I hate that backwards home known as the sky.
But thanks to planes, God's rays won't slay my eyes.

Why Don't We Talk About Blankets?

Blankets are weird.
Brilliant,
Blue,
Black,
or
Bland, Blankets are soft skins.

They're fur for
Frail
And
Frightening
Souls at night time.

They calm, soothe, and protect.
And,
They remind me of
when

I was ten…

When I Noticed Those Kahones.

Although I don't know a thing about Kahones,
They show up almost everywhere I go.

At Calvary Chapel church,
As my dad smacked puny Jesus-screaming drums,
Some twenties blondie punched a mostly broken black Kahone.

At my grueling barely Baptist private high school,
As my white elitist supposedly-pristine choir-peers tried soul songs,
Some strangely-good-at-singing jock-teen poked a preppy wood-
stained Kahone
Owned by an overly wealthy faculty-puppet-mastering family.

And tonight

At my Christian College's weekly comedically boring preaching,
As I write my tiny dopey devotions and poems,
I am eyeing a quiet humanity-abandoned lipsticky-red Kahone
Lacking anything remotely unique or interesting.

And yet, I don't know why,

But I feel sorry for this solitary crimson little guy,
He may only be a plain lame-excuse-for-a-music-box song-repository,
But he still deserves as much attention as anyone or anything.

Although I don't know a thing about Kahones,
I want to take this lonely squarey buddy home

Since I swear this silly tiny empty silent red little thing
Has an identity.

And, I swear,

Kahones just like it
Have been showing up everywhere
Just so someone like me
could finally see
their animacy.

Dreamer.

"Dreams bleed peace."

Each week, priests
preached bleak creeds.
"Dreams freeze drinks.
Dreams grease teens.
Deeds lead clean
teens." These weeds
teased glee. These
fiends reamed me.

Dreams freed me.

Viewing That Vent on Sunday.

That vent popped out as I viewed through that window since
it had fun characteristics that made me wince
at first but grew on me, like its boldness, which showed
as it flashed me with rusty lines. It clearly glowed

PURE WHITE ONCE. Folly came with age. But,
IT IS PROUD despite the crust because
IT STILL FLARES white here and there. It still
SHINES WITH DIRT. The orange might have killed

Its innocence, but it replaced it with
experience and skill. That vent is stiff,
but younger, looser, fresh vents flop off dead
From harsh air while that old vent lies in bed.

I hope I see that vent again someday
blowing, glowing,
making me smile
On Sunday.

Grey.

One day, you'll wonder what God has to say
About a topic. So, you'll search all day
In Scripture. When that sadly fails, you'll pray
Until you realize that topic is Grey.

It's an undead blob that crawls without stall.
No one can stop its goopy, slimy, tall,
And massive body. But, don't skip its call
Or it'll smash your faith into a wall.

To understand Grey topics, submit to
God. Though discovery might not ensue,
Your faith'll strengthen since God'll help you
Make peace with Grey, and that's all we can do.

Presence.

I need to be here.
I need them to see
My eyes and their tears
And their lack of glee.

I give them my eyes.
They must give me theirs,
For sight cannot lie.
Truth shows in one's stare.

"Know that I'm alive,"
I scream and they hear.
"My words must survive."
Their death is my fear.

We all need that one,
Who rescues our soul,
Who, when we are done,
Takes back what death stole.

Do You Need Fame?

You don't need praise.
You don't need esteemed movies or plays.
You don't even need socially revered blessings,
like love or security.
Ultimately, you only need to be happy,
even if only occasionally.

Peace.

I'm looking for Peace,
Something scarcely seen.
With that, Fear will cease,
That powerful friend,

Who invades your thoughts
With his mocking peers.
With them, your mind rots
As they laugh and sneer.

Peace ends this fight
With a steadfast truce.
And, despite its might,
Fear stops running loose.

Fear will still exist.
It's life's greatest friend.
But if Peace persists,
Fear won't be our end.

Do You Have a Minute?

Hello, sweet reader! How are you today?
Ecstatic? Happy? Bored? Exhausted? Dead?
Do sinking thoughts cremate your cautious head?
What tyrant tasks direct your disarray?
Alright, Alright. I'm done with this display.
Most poets' reader questions go unsaid.
I'm sorry if these gave you any dread,
but I just wanted to say: it's okay.

No matter what invades your day or life,
I know you'll conquer it. Do you know why?
Because you try. You read my poem through.
You have the gall to fight despite your strife,
which means one day, if not today, you'll fly.
Goodbye, sweet reader. I believe in you!